ANNO REGNI

GEORGII III.

REGIS

Magnæ Britanniæ, Franciæ, & Hiberniæ,

DECIMO NONO.

At the Parliament begun and holden at *Westminster*, the Twenty-ninth Day of *November*, *Anno Domini* 1774, in the Fifteenth Year of the Reign of our Sovereign Lord GEORGE the Third, by the Grace of God, of *Great Britain*, *France*, and *Ireland*, King, Defender of the Faith, *&c.*

And from thence continued, by several Prorogations, to the Twenty-sixth Day of *November*, 1778; being the Fifth Session of the Fourteenth Parliament of *Great Britain*.

LONDON:
Printed by CHARLES EYRE and WILLIAM STRAHAN,
Printers to the King's most Excellent Majesty. 1779.

ANNO DECIMO NONO

Georgii III. Regis.

C A P. XLVI.

An Act for building a new Gaol and House of Correction for the County of *Pembroke*.

WHEREAS the Common Gaol of the County of Pembroke, situate in the Town and County of Haverfordwest, is greatly too small, inconvenient, and unsafe, and is situate in a low, unhealthy, and confined Situation, and being a very ancient Building is greatly gone to Decay, and is so incapable of being repaired in a proper Manner, that it is necessary a new Gaol should be built: And whereas the Justices of the Peace for the County of Pembroke, at their last Epiphany Quarter Sessions, held on the Thirteenth Day of January, One thousand seven hundred and seventy-nine, ordered that Hugh Owen, John Wogan, William Williams, Hugh Savage, Esquires, James Evans and William Holcombe, Clerks, be appointed to treat with Robert Prust Esquire, for the absolute Purchase of the Castle of Haverfordwest, in order to erect a Com-

Preamble.

mon Gaol therein; and, that in case they could not agree with him, to treat with some other Person or Persons for a Piece of Ground for erecting a County Gaol thereon: And whereas the building a new Gaol, and also an House of Correction, for the said County of Pembroke, within the said Castle of Haverfordwest, or in some other convenient and healthy Situation within the said Town of Haverfordwest, or elsewhere within the said County of Pembroke, will tend greatly to the Safety and Health of Persons confined therein, and be of publick Utility: May it therefore please Your Majesty that it may be enacted; and be it enacted by the King's most Excellent Majesty, by and with the Advice and Consent of the Lords Spiritual and Temporal, and Commons, in this present Parliament assembled, and by the Authority of the same, That it shall and may be lawful to and for the Justices of the Peace for the said County of Pembroke, at their next General or Quarter Sessions of the Peace, or at any other Special Sessions to be holden for the said County after the passing of this Act, or at any other subsequent General Quarter Sessions, or other Sessions as aforesaid, to authorise One or more Person or Persons, on their Behalf, to contract for and purchase the said Castle of Haverfordwest, or some other convenient Piece or Pieces of Ground, Tenements or Hereditaments, either within the Town and County of Haverfordwest, or elsewhere within the said County of Pembroke; and that the same, when purchased, shall be conveyed to the Right Honourable Richard Lord Milford, the Right Honourable William Lord Kensington, Sir William Owen Baronet, Hugh Owen Esquire, John Campbell Esquire, John Symmons Esquire, John Harries of Crigglas Esquire, William Ford Esquire, John Bartlett Allen Esquire, John Harries of Priskilly Esquire, John Wogan Esquire, Thomas Kymer Esquire, Hugh Owen Esquire, George Bowen Esquire, Stephen Colby Esquire, Thomas Colby Esquire, Thomas Lloyd of Cumgloyne Esquire, John Tucker Esquire, Gwynne Vaughan Esquire, George Harries of Tregwint Esquire, George Roch of Clareston Esquire, Barrett Bown Jordan Esquire, Hugh Savage Esquire, William Williams of Ivy Tower Esquire,

John

Cap. 46.   GEORGII III. REGIS.   993

John Poyer Esquire, Evan Griffiths Esquire, and William Jones Esquire, William Holcombe Clerk, John Jordan Clerk, John Roch Clerk, and James Evans Clerk, and the Survivors of them, and their Heirs, who shall be seised thereof in Trust for the Service and Benefit of the said County, for the Uses herein-after mentioned.

And be it further enacted, That it shall be lawful for all Persons whatsoever, seised of, interested in, or intitled unto the said Castle of Haverfordwest, or unto such other Piece or Pieces of Ground, Tenements, or Hereditaments, and also for all Bodies Politick, Corporate, or Collegiate, Corporations Aggregate or Sole, Husbands, Guardians, Trustees, and Feoffees in Trust, Committees, Executors, Administrators, and all other Trustees whatsoever, not only for and on Behalf of themselves, but also for and on Behalf of their Cestuique Trusts, whether Infants or Issue unborn, Lunaticks, Idiots, Femes-covert, or other Person or Persons whatsoever, and to and for all Femes-covert who are or shall be seised or interested in their own Right, and to and for all and every Person and Persons whomsoever who are or shall be seised, possessed of, or interested in, the said Castle of Haverfordwest, or in such other Piece or Pieces of Ground, Tenements or Hereditaments, under any Manner of Right or Title whatsoever, to convey the same respectively unto them the said Trustees herein-before named, and the Survivors of them, and their Heirs, for the Purpose of building a new Gaol and House of Correction for the said County of Pembroke; and in case the said Justices and Persons cannot agree upon a Sum to be paid for any of the Premises respectively, then the said Justices shall cause the Value of the said Estates to be enquired into and ascertained by a Jury of Twelve indifferent Men of the County of Pembroke; and in order thereto, the said Justices, or the major Part of them so assembled, are hereby empowered and required, from Time to Time, as Occasion shall be, to summon and call before such Jury and examine upon Oath all and every Person and Persons whomsoever who

Incapacitated Persons impowered to sell Lands, &c.

If Parties cannot agree, Jury to settle the Recompence.

Witnesses may be examined on Oath.

who shall be thought necessary and proper to be examined concerning the Premises, (which Oath any Two or more of such Justices are hereby empowered to administer), and such Justices shall, by ordering a View or otherwise, use all lawful Ways and Means, as well for their own as for the said Jury's Information in the Premises; and after the said Jury shall have enquired of and assessed such Value and Recompence, they the said Justices shall thereupon adjudge the Sum or Sums of Money, so assessed by the said Jury, to be paid to the said Person or Persons according to the Verdict of such Jury, *Verdict of Jury to be final.* which said Verdict shall be final, binding and conclusive, to all Intents and Purposes whatsoever, against all Parties and Persons whomsoever: And for summoning and returning such Juries, the said Justices are hereby empowered to issue their Warrant or Warrants to the Sheriff of the County of Pembroke, commanding him to impannel, summon, and return, an indifferent Jury of Twenty-four Men of the said County, but not being in the Commission of the Peace, to appear before the said Justices at such Time and Place as in such Warrant or *Sheriff to summon a Jury.* Warrants shall be appointed; and such Sheriff or his Deputy or Deputies is and are hereby required to impannel, summon, and return, such Number of Persons accordingly, and out of the Persons so impannelled, summoned, and returned, or out of such of them as shall appear upon such Summons, the said Justices shall, and they are hereby impowered and required to swear or cause to be sworn Twelve Men, who shall be the Jury for the Purposes aforesaid; and in Default of a sufficient Number of Jurymen, the said Sheriff, or his Deputy or Deputies, shall return other honest and indifferent Men, not being in the Commission of the Peace, either of the Standers-by, or that speedily can be procured to attend *Jurors may be challenged.* that Service, to the Number of Twelve; and all Persons concerned shall have their lawful Challenges against any of the said Jurymen when they come to be sworn, *Justices may impose a Fine on Sheriff, &c. making Default.* but shall not challenge the Array; and the said Justices shall have Power, from Time to Time, to impose any reasonable Fine or Fines on such Sheriff, his Deputy or Deputies,

Deputies, Bailiffs or Agents, making Default in the Premises, and on any of the Persons that shall be summoned and returned on such Jury and shall not appear, or that shall refuse to be sworn on the said Jury, or being so sworn shall refuse to give, or not giving their Verdict, or in any other Manner wilfully neglecting their Duty therein, contrary to the true Intent and Meaning of this Act; and on any of the Persons who being required to give Evidence before the said Jury shall refuse or neglect to appear, or appearing shall refuse to be examined or to give Evidence; and which Fine or Fines shall not exceed the Sum of Five Pounds upon any One Person, and shall be recovered by Distress and Sale of the Offender's Goods and Chattels, by Warrant or Warrants under the Hands and Seals of any Two or more of such Justices, and shall be applied for the Purposes of this Act.

And be it further enacted, That upon Payment of the Money so agreed to be paid for such Purposes, or to be assessed as aforesaid, or upon Tender thereof to such Persons as aforesaid, or to their Agents, and in case of Want of Opportunity to tender, or of Refusal to accept the same, then upon leaving the same in the Hands of the Clerk of the Peace for the County of Pembroke, to be by him applied to and for the Use of such Person and Persons as the said Justices, or the major Part of them, so assembled as aforesaid, shall order, direct, and appoint, it shall be lawful for the said Justices, their Surveyors, Workmen, or Agents, to take Possession of the said Castle of Haverfordwest, or such other Piece or Pieces of Ground, Tenements, and Hereditaments; and that the Whole of the said Castle, or such other Ground, Tenements, and Hereditaments, and every Part thereof, shall be, and the same are hereby declared to be vested in the said Trustees herein-before named, and the Survivors of them, and their Heirs, for the Purpose of building, erecting, and making a Common Gaol and House of Correction for the said County of Pembroke for the Confinement of Criminals, Debtors, and others, and also a proper Place for the Residence of the Gaoler, and such other Conveniencies as may be necessary.

On Payment or Tender of Money, Premises to be vested in Trustees;

for the Purpose of building a new Gaol.

Provided

For saving of Rents to the Duke of *Leeds*.

Provided always, and be it enacted by the Authority aforesaid, That nothing in this Act contained shall extend, or be construed to extend, to affect any Right or Claim of the most Noble Thomas Duke of Leeds, his Heirs or Assigns, of, in, or to, any annual or Fee-farm Rent or Fee-farm Rents, or any other Rights, Dues, or Payments, issuing out of, or reserved or payable for, the Castle and Lordship of Haverfordwest, in the said County of Pembroke, or out of or for the same alone, or together with any other Castles, Lordships, Lands, Tenements, or Hereditaments whatsoever, which shall or may be purchased for the Purposes of this Act; but that the said Castle and Lordship of Haverfordwest, and every or any other Castles, Lordships, Lands, Tenements, and Hereditaments whatsoever, and every Part thereof, shall still continue liable to and chargeable with the same, in such and the same Manner as if this Act had not been made; any Thing in this Act contained to the contrary thereof notwithstanding.

New Trustees how to be chosen.

And be it further enacted, That when and as often as the said Trustees shall be reduced by Death to the Number of Five, then it shall and may be lawful to and for the remaining Trustees, or the Majority of them, to elect and appoint, by Writing under their Hands and Seals, any Number of Persons residing in the said County, so as the Trustees so to be elected, together with the remaining Trustees, do not exceed the Number of Thirty-one, in whom, together with the old Trustees, the Fee-simple and Inheritance of the said Castle of Haverfordwest, or such other Piece or Pieces of Ground, Tenements, or Hereditaments, so to be purchased as aforesaid, shall, by virtue of such Appointment, be vested in Trust for the Service and Benefit of the said County for the Purposes aforesaid; and the said Number of Trustees shall, from Time to Time, be filled up in Manner aforesaid, whenever the Trustees shall be reduced to the Number of Five.

Power to build a new County Gaol.

And be it further enacted, That when the said Castle of Haverfordwest, or such other Piece or Pieces of Ground, Tenements, or Hereditaments, shall be purchased;

chased; it shall and may be lawful for the said Justices to cause to be built, erected, made, and finished thereon, a convenient Gaol and House of Correction, for the Confinement of Criminals, Debtors, and others; and also a proper Place for the Residence of the Gaoler, and such other Buildings and Conveniencies as shall be adjudged requisite by the said Justices at their said General Quarter Sessions, or at any other Sessions as aforesaid, for the safe keeping of such Persons as shall be committed to the same, either for Debt, Felony, or any other Offence; which Gaol and House of Correction, when built and finished, is hereby declared to be a publick and common Gaol and House of Correction for the said County of Pembroke; and shall from Time to Time be maintained, supported, and repaired, by such Ways and Means as other Gaols and Houses of Correction in this Kingdom are by Law to be maintained, supported, and repaired; and the Sheriff of the said County of Pembroke, for the Time being, shall have the keeping thereof; and shall have Power, when the said Gaol is made fit for the Reception and Safe-keeping of Prisoners, to remove thither all such Prisoners as shall then be in his Custody, which Removal shall not be deemed or taken to be an Escape.

And be it further enacted, That the Ground, or Scite, whereon the said new Gaol and House of Correction shall be built, or thereto belonging or appertaining, if the same shall be within the Town and County of Haverfordwest, shall immediately, from and after the same shall be purchased, by virtue of this Act, be for ever exempted and separated from the said Town and County of Haverfordwest, in the same Manner as the said old Gaol now is, and shall for ever thereafter be, and be deemed to be, Part of the County of Pembroke; any Law, Act, Statute, Provision, Charter, Custom, or Ordinance, or any Thing herein contained, to the contrary notwithstanding. *New Gaol to be deemed Part of the County of Pembroke.*

Provided also, and be it further enacted, That it shall and may be lawful to and for the Sheriff of the County of Pembroke for the Time being, and his Agents, Officers, *Sheriff to have the same Privileges as formerly.*

cers, and Assistants, from Time to Time, and at all Times, to convey Prisoners to and from the said intended new Gaol or House of Correction, if the same shall be built in the Town and County of Haverfordwest, through the said Town and County; and have, use, and exercise, all such other Privileges and Customs as have been heretofore used and exercised or claimed by Sheriffs of the County of Pembroke, in respect to the old Gaol; any Thing herein contained to the contrary notwithstanding.

When the new Gaol is completed, the old Gaol shall revert to the Town and County of Haverfordwest.

And be it further enacted, That from and immediately after the said new Gaol and House of Correction shall be completed and finished, and the Prisoners removed from the old Gaol, the Possession of the old Gaol shall be taken by or delivered to the Corporation of the said Town of Haverfordwest, and that from thenceforth the same, and the Ground or Scite belonging thereto, shall be no longer exempted and separated from the said Town and County of Haverfordwest as heretofore, but shall from thenceforth be and be deemed to be Part of the said Town and County of Haverfordwest, and not Part of the County of Pembroke; and that then and from thenceforth all Rents, Dues, and Payments whatsoever, heretofore charged upon, or payable or paid by the said County of Pembroke for the same, shall cease, determine, and be no longer paid or payable; any Law, Act, Statute, Provision, Charter, Custom, or Ordinance, or any Thing herein contained, to the contrary notwithstanding.

Justices in Sessions impowered to raise 2,000 l. for the Purposes of this Act.

And, for raising Money to purchase the said Castle, or such other Ground, Tenements, or Hereditaments, proper and sufficient for the Purposes of this Act, and for the building, erecting, making, and finishing such new Gaol and House of Correction, and Buildings as aforesaid, and other the Purposes of this Act; be it enacted by the Authority aforesaid, That it shall and may be lawful to and for the Justices of the Peace for the said County of Pembroke, at their next General or Quarter Sessions to be held for the said County after the passing of this Act, or at any subsequent General or Quarter Sessions,

Sessions, to conclude and agree upon, and to assess such Sum and Sums of Money, as they shall from Time to Time find necessary for the Purposes of this Act, so as the Whole of such Assessments shall not exceed the Sum of Two thousand Pounds; and the same shall be rated and assessed in such and the same Manner, and according to such and the same Proportions, upon every Town, Parish, Hamlet, or Place, within the Limits of the said County of Pembroke, and upon the Boroughs, Towns Corporate, and all other Precincts and Liberties within the said County, and be collected, received, levied, and paid, and be accounted for by the Persons making such Collections, in such Manner, and by such Means, with such Power of levying and for enforcing the Collection and Payment thereof, and for punishing all Persons whose Duty it shall be to collect or account for the same, and shall make Default therein, as the County Rates have been usually, or may, by an Act made in the Twelfth Year of the Reign of his late Majesty, intituled, An Act for the more easy assessing, collecting, and levying, of County Rates; or by any other Act or Acts of Parliament, be assessed, collected, received, levied, paid, and accounted for, within the said County of Pembroke; and such Assessments, when received, shall be from Time to Time paid, by the Treasurer or Treasurers of the said County, to the said Justices so assembled as aforesaid, or to such Person or Persons as they shall, by Order of Court, appoint to receive the same; and the Receipt of such Justices, or of such Person or Persons as shall be so appointed, shall be a full and sufficient Discharge to such Treasurer or Treasurers, for the Payment of such Monies.

And be it further enacted, That the several and respective parochial Officers, or other Persons, who shall pay, or be liable to pay, the Rates or Assessments which shall be made and rated, for the Purposes of this Act, upon any Parish, Town, Borough, Liberty, or Place; and also all such parochial Officers and Persons, upon whom any such Rates or Assessments shall be levied, shall and may from Time to Time, after Notice shall be given

Officers paying the Rates may assess the same.

of the Amount of the Rate or Assessment upon such Town, Parish, or Place, either before the Payment thereof, by such parochial Officers or persons, or after the same shall have been actually paid by, or levied upon, such Officers or Persons, rate and levy such Monies, by a separate and distinct Rate and Assessment, upon every such respective Town, Parish, Town Corporate, or Place, in such Manner and Proportion, and with such Powers for recovering thereof, as any other County Rate may be assessed or levied.

Magistrates in distinct Jurisdictions to make Assessments.

And whereas there are some Boroughs, Towns Corporate, Liberties, and other distinct Jurisdictions, within the County of Pembroke aforesaid, in which the Justices, acting in the Commission of the Peace of the said County, have no Power or Authority, be it therefore enacted, That the Justices, or other Magistrates, acting in and for the Boroughs, Towns Corporate, Liberties, and other distinct Jurisdictions aforesaid, shall assess a Sum or Sums of Money, in the same Proportion as the Justices of the County shall assess Monies for the Purposes of this Act, and in like Manner, when collected and received, shall pay the same to the Treasurer or Treasurers of the County aforesaid, who shall account for it to the Justices of the County in the same Manner as for the Money received in the County at large; and that nothing in this Act shall give the Justices of the County any Power or Authority in the Boroughs, Towns Corporate, Liberties, or other distinct Jurisdictions, which they had not before.

Application of Money.

And be it further enacted, That all such Charges and Expences as have been, or shall be sustained or expended in or about procuring this present Act of Parliament, shall (in the first Place) be satisfied and paid out of the Monies to be raised by virtue or in pursuance of this Act; and that after such Charges and Expences, and the Charges of erecting, building, making, completing, and finishing the said new Gaol, and House of Correction, and Buildings, and all Debts incurred thereby, and all other Monies to be paid in pursuance of this Act, shall be fully paid and satisfied, the Surplus of the Monies to be be raised and levied by virtue of this Act shall, by Order of the said Justices, assembled in their General or Quarter Sessions as aforesaid, be paid into the Publick Stock of the said County, and be deemed and taken, and shall and may be applied and paid, as Part of the Common Stock, to and for such Uses as the County Stock can or may be applied.

Provided always, and be it further enacted, That in case all the Charges and Expences of obtaining and passing this Act shall not be paid within Three Calendar Months next after the passing of the same, the Treasurer of the said County of Pembroke shall, and is hereby required, within One Calendar Month after the Expiration of the said Three Calendar Months, to pay and defray all such Charges and Expences; and the said Justices are hereby authorized and required to allow the same in the said Treasurer's Accounts. *Expences of this Act how to be paid.*

And be it further enacted, That some Time between Michaelmas and Christmas in every Year, a fair and just Account shall, by Order of the said Justices, or the major Part of them, assembled as aforesaid, be made and wrote out of all the Monies received and paid by virtue and in pursuance of this Act, and how, and to whom, and when, and for what Purposes, the same have been laid out, paid, and expended; a Copy or Duplicate of which Account, signed by the said Justices, or the major Part of them, so assembled as aforesaid, shall be deposited with the Clerk of the Peace for the said County of Pembroke for the Time being, to be kept among the Records of the Sessions of the Peace there, who shall permit any Person so taxed as aforesaid to inspect the same at all seasonable Times, paying Sixpence for such Inspection, and shall, upon Demand, forthwith give Copies of the same, or any Part thereof, to such Persons, paying at the Rate of Sixpence for every One hundred Words, and so in Proportion for any greater or lesser Number of Words. *Accounts to be made up annually.*

Provided always, and be it further enacted, That all Persons who shall apprehend themselves overcharged, or otherwise aggrieved, by any Assessment, or other Act, to be *Persons aggrieved may appeal to the Quarter Sessions.*

be made or done by virtue of this present Act, may appeal to the Justices of the Peace assembled at their next Quarter Sessions to be held for the said County after Demand of the Monies assessed, or after such other Act done; who shall and may make such Order therein as to them, or the major Part of them there and then present, shall seem meet.

<small>Limitation of Actions.</small>

And be it further enacted, That if any Action or Suit shall be brought or commenced against any Person or Persons, for any Thing done in pursuance of this Act, such Action or Suit shall be brought and commenced within Three Calendar Months next after the Fact committed, and not afterwards, and shall be laid and brought in the County of Pembroke, and not elsewhere; and the Defendant or Defendants, in such Action or Suit, shall and may plead the General Issue, and give this Act and the special Matter in Evidence at any Trial to be had thereupon; and if the Plaintiff or Plaintiffs shall become nonsuit, or discontinue such Action or Suit, or if, upon Demurrer, Judgement shall be given against the Plaintiff or Plaintiffs, the Defendant or Defendants shall and may recover Treble Costs, and have such Remedy for such Costs as any other Defendant or Defendants hath or have for Costs in any other Cases by Law.

<small>General Issue.</small>

<small>Treble Costs.</small>

<small>Publick Act.</small>

And be it further enacted, That this Act shall be deemed and taken to be a Publick Act; and all Judges, Justices, and other Persons, shall take Notice thereof as such, without specially pleading the same.

FINIS.

blank

blank

blank

blank

blank

blank

blank

blank

www.ingramcontent.com/pod-product-compliance
Lightning Source LLC
Chambersburg PA
CBHW082225220526
45470CB00010B/3311